Finding Birds in

I can't believe it's actually 20 years since I wrote the fi was perhaps the most popular foreign destination for t get-togethers arranged by the late and greatly missed now and I'm not sure why. It's still a great place for r.   ...- -µ----......-> sucn as Black Vulture, Eleonora's Falcon, Audouin's Gull and Moustached Warbler are still there. Indeed, you would think that recent taxonomic changes would have made Mallorca even more attractive as it's the best place to find recent 'splits' such as Balearic Warbler, Balearic Shearwater and, soon, Moltoni's (Subalpine) Warbler. Also there are now even more birds to see, as the island has been colonised naturally by Marbled Ducks, Griffon Vultures and Great White Egrets and, with more than a little help, by Purple Swamphen, Red-Crested Pochard and Red-knobbed Coot.

So, although other birdwatching guides have been published since 1991, notably one by Graham Hearl, and another 'Birding Tourist's Guide to Mallorca' by a co-operative of Mallorcan birders, I feel this completely revised version of my book is greatly needed. It updates most of the sites in the original book and adds several new sites from the 'Tourist's Guide' and a couple of others not previously mentioned elsewhere. As ever, the aim is not just to point out general areas where you might see birds but to show you EXACTLY where to go to find birds like Balearic Warbler, Moltoni's Warbler, Red-knobbed Coot, Red-footed Falcon and Moustached Warbler.

You can get an even better idea of what many of these sites are like by watching our DVD of the same title and you can help to keep the book up to date by contributing to the free app 'Finding Birds: the latest gen' which is available for any computer and most smartphones via the apps page of our website www.easybirder.co.uk.

What struck me most about returning to Mallorca after so many years is that I'd forgotten what a really beautiful island it is; arguably more appealing as a holiday destination than any site in mainland Spain or Portugal and just the sort of place where a birder can take non-birding family members and everyone will have a good time.

Dave Gosney, July 2012

Acknowledgements

When planning my latest visit, I found that the most useful source of new information was the excellent forum on Mallorca at www.birdforum.net that is kept up to date by local birder Mike Montier. Mike provides a great service of answering questions from would-be visitors and the forum also provides a place where recent sightings can be posted. I'm also grateful to everyone who has written to me to help me update the original book, especially Hilary MacBean and Steve Hearn whose information is included here. On behalf of everyone who visits Mallorca I feel I should thank the visionaries such as Eddie Watkinson, Pat Bishop and Graham Hearl not only for providing visitors with endless help and advice but also for their part in establishing nature reserves on the island. One wonders whether the Albufera, for example, would be anything like the attraction, to birds and birders, that it currently is if it hadn't been for their determination to protect it from development. Good luck to the Mallorcan birders who now continue to build on their legacy. Lastly of course I need to thank my partner, Liz for doing such a fine job of producing the DVD to go with this book and for being the most delightful companion on trips such as this.

s'Albufera

Attraction

Quite simply one of the best wetlands in the Mediterranean and certainly the best on any of the islands. Highlights include up to 100 Eleonora's Falcons hunting, 800 pairs of Moustached Warbler (the biggest population in Spain), recently established populations of Purple Swamphen, Marbled Duck and Red-knobbed Coot and superb viewing facilities overlooking pools that attract passing waders, herons, ducks and terns.

Getting there

The main entrance is off the Alcudia-C'an Picafort road. Drive along the main road through Alcudia, following signs to Arta, until you see an obvious bridge (English Bridge). Just beyond this is a roundabout with a right-turn, signposted to S'Albufera reserve, which leads to the main car park (39.7991N, 3.1191E). The area can also be accessed via the C'an Picafort-Muro road (see site 14) and via the Alcudia-Sa Pobla road (see site 11)

Access

It is no longer possible to drive to the information centre so you'll need to walk 1.25 km from the car park. There is no access to some of the tracks described in my earlier book – please keep to the tracks shown here. All visitors are asked to visit the centre to obtain a permit (free); this helps to demonstrate the number of people using the reserve so you should ensure you get yourself counted. From April to October the reserve is open from 8am-6pm. If you wish to visit outside of these hours, ask for permission at the information centre (it was granted to us with no problem). The entrance gate is locked at 6pm but there is a gap in the wall that still allows pedestrian access.

Notes

1. It is no longer necessary to look for roosting Night Herons in the pines near the car park because they are usually visible further down the track in the bushes overhanging the main channel. Look for a little path on the right, parallel to the main track and view the herons from there (eg 39.7992N, 3.1142E); 1-3 are usually visible.

2. Closer to the visitor centre there is a raised boardwalk beside the main track. From here you can listen for Great Reed and Moustached Warbler. The latter species is often silent by day but becomes more vocal after 8pm when the bushes alongside the boardwalk are busy with noisy Cattle Egrets nesting by the main channel. Night Herons fly around at that time too and in 2012 there was also a singing Savi's Warbler audible from the boardwalk.

3. The main channel (39.7976N, 3.1057E) close to the visitor centre has breeding Purple Swamphen, Red-knobbed Coot and Red-crested Pochard, all established following a re-introduction programme. In spring, the whole area is alive with Nightingales and Cetti's Warblers. The main bridge over the channel is said to be good for seeing Little Bittern, though not in my experience.

4. The pools closest to the information centre (Sa Roca pools) are overlooked by two hides from which you can get exceptionally close views of ducks and, especially, waders. On passage, Little Stint, Wood Sandpiper, Curlew Sandpiper and Spotted Redshank can all be expected and Marsh Sandpiper and Temminck's Stint are regularly seen. You may get your best views of Swamphen from these hides and this is probably the best bet for seeing Marbled Duck too; following a natural recolonisation from the Spanish mainland, small numbers are regularly present but not always in view.

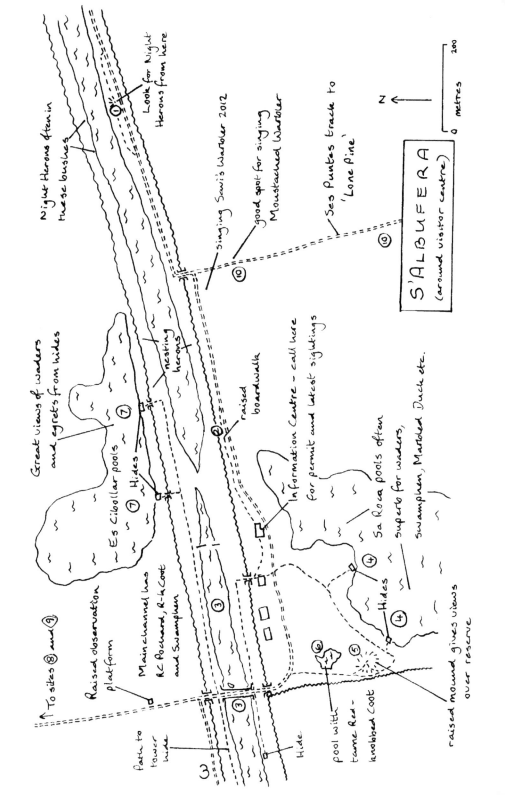

S'ALBUFERA
(around visitor centre)

Night Herons often in these bushes

Look for Night Herons from here

Singing Savi's Warbler 2012

good spot for singing Moustached Warbler

Ses Puntes track to 'Lone Pine'

N

0   metres   200

Great views of waders and egrets from hides

nesting herons

raised boardwalk

Es Cibollar pools

Hides

Information Centre – call here for permit and latest sightings

Sa Roca pools often superb for waders, swamphen, Marbled Duck etc.

To sites ⑧ and ⑨

Raised observation platform

Main channel has RC Pochard, R-k Coot and Swamphen

Path to tower hide

Hide

pool with tame Red-knobbed Coot

raised mound gives views over reserve

Hides

5. A nature trail close to the centre leads to a raised mound (39.7956N, 3.1045E) which provides a good view of the reserve. This is one of several places from which you can look for birds such as Marsh Harrier, Osprey, Purple Heron and, in spring, Eleonora's Falcon.

6. Next to the mound is a little pool (39.7961N, 3.1044E) with a noticeboard illustrating the species that have been reintroduced to the reserve. The White-headed Ducks seem to have disappeared from the reserve but the other species are successfully breeding, including Red-knobbed Coots which are so tame around this pond they will come to you as if for food even though all visitors are asked not to feed the birds. Some of them are daubed with big white plastic collars but others are unadorned and more photogenic (and tickable-looking)

7. A signposted nature trail continues to two more hides (Es Cibollar I and II) overlooking pools (Es Cibollar) to the north of the main channel. In spring 2012, the water levels here were a little too high but the pools were still good for stilts, egrets, swamphens and various shanks and sandpipers. The islands also have nesting Stone Curlews which put on noisy shows at dusk. The Cattle Egret colony, presumably with Night Herons and Little Egrets in there too, is just beyond the end of the footpath to the second hide. Please keep to the path.

8. From the main bridge you can walk northward for 1.1 km passing more pools on your right. The reeds beside the path tend to be less tall so you have a better chance here of seeing the reedbed warblers, especially Moustached Warbler. In April 2012 the most reliable place for seeing this common but elusive species was from the 2nd observation platform on the right (approx 39.8043N, 3.1026E), 750 metres from the bridge. They seem to prefer areas of younger reed but when they do sing they will perch prominently on taller reeds. The song is reminiscent of Reed Warbler but is sweeter, faster and has a 'tinkling' quality. A rising 'lu,lu,lu...' is distinctive but not always given at the beginning of the song.

9. About 300 metres further on, a path to the left (39.8073N, 3.1018E) leads to another hide overlooking the Es Colombars pools. In spring when water levels are typically high, the main attraction here is that you often get views of the local Ospreys, either fishing the pools or eating their prey on one of the poles between the hide and the background power station. In autumn, when other pools have dried out, this will often be the best place for waders.

10. Another good area for looking for Moustached Warbler is along the Ses Puntes track which leads south towards the Depuradora (site 15), though there is no public access connecting the two sites. This track features two viewing platforms, the first of which, opposite a stand of pine trees overlooks 'Lone Pine pools' which can be great for waders.

11. To access the western side of the reserve, follow signs in Alcudia to Sa Pobla. After passing the power station on your right, the road makes 2 sharp bends either side of the bridge at km post 5. You can park near the bridge and walk east (from 39.7961N, 3.0729E), back towards the information centre. En route you will reach an observation tower (39.7957N, 3.0921E) which offers probably the best view of the reserve. This is the place to visit at dawn or dusk in spring to look for feeding flocks of Eleonora's Falcon; over 100 have been counted from here. Although the falcons begin to arrive in late April and remain until early October, the best time to see them over the marsh is in May. Looking north from the tower you get distant views of the Purple Heron colony. On the nearby main channel there are usually Red-crested Pochard and Gadwall. In late April 2012, we also had a Moustached Warbler in reeds to the north, a pair of Red-knobbed Coot on the channel and several Night Herons flying over. However, we failed to see the Little Bittern which have been described as 'guaranteed to give good views from late March onward' (Hearl 1999).

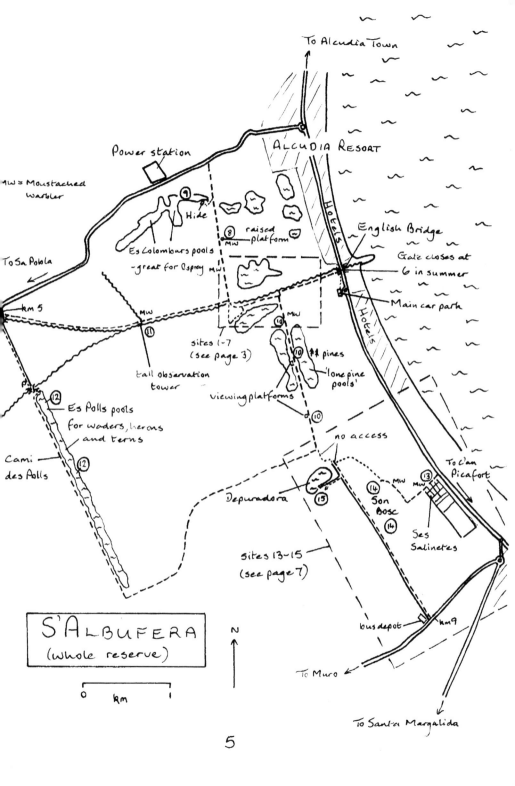

To Alcudia Town

ALCUDIA RESORT

Power station

MW = Moustached Warbler

Hide

Es Colombars pools
— great for Osprey MW

raised platform
MW

8

7

To Sa Pobla

km 5

MW

11

sites 1–7
(see page 3)

tall observation tower

viewing platforms

10 MW

10 ♯♯ pines

10 'lone pine pools'

10

English Bridge

Gate closes at 6 in summer

Main car park

Hotels

Hotels

To Can Picafort

P

12

Es Polls pools
for waders, herons
and terns

Cami
des Polls

12

12

no access

Depuradora

15

14 Son Bosc

14

MW MW

13

Ses Salinetes

sites 13–15
(see page 7)

bus depot km 9

To Muro

To Santa Margalida

S'ALBUFERA
(whole reserve)

N

0   km   1

5

12.   Where the road bends sharply right after the bridge, a track (39.7954N, 3.0732E) continues southward. It is possible to drive down that track for 800 metres and park (39.7889N, 3.0773E) before you reach another bridge. The reeds here are very tall but good for Great Reed Warblers and the bushes by this bridge are great for Cetti's Warblers and Nightingales. However, the main reason for visiting this site is to walk beyond the bridge to check an area of pools beside a track called the Cami des Polls. Amongst the breeding stilts and plovers there are often some passage waders and this is one of the best places to see birds such as Squacco Heron, Glossy Ibis, Collared Pratincole and Whiskered Tern. The pools can be viewed from a gate (39.7885N, 3.0776E) just 50 metres from where you park the car so it makes a much more convenient place for a brief visit than the pools around the visitor centre.

13.   Another good spot for both Great Reed and Moustached Warblers is the track past the old saltpans (Ses Salinetes) at the south end of the reserve. To get there, continue south from English Bridge and look for a broad driveway (39.7795N, 3.1321E) on the right after 2.6 km. Park next to the sign saying 's'Illot' and walk from here. The pools themselves usually have a small but varied selection of waders, herons and ducks including, sometimes, Marbled Duck. After 500 metres, the track bends sharply right. In front of you is the area known as Son Bosc (site 14) giving you another chance to look for Bee-eater, Short-toed Lark and Tawny Pipit. The track to the right gives views over Son Bosc on the left and the reedbeds on the right but then degenerates into a path which ceases to be productive and ends at a fence which prevents you continuing to the Depuradora (site 15).

14.   In the past it has been possible to explore the Son Bosc area (39.7774N, 3.1228E) in search of breeding Bee-eaters but this area is now fenced off. However, the key species can still be seen from the road to the Depuradora. To get there, continue south towards C'an Picafort but turn right at each of two roundabouts, following signs to Muro. After 1 km, turn right again just after the km 9 post, before a bus depot on the right (39.7648N, 3.1312E). Drive slowly, looking and listening for Short-toed Lark, Tawny Pipit, Thekla Lark and Bee-eater and check the many fences for migrants such as chats and shrikes. The map shows where the key species were found in 2012. Many of the 'sandhills' are now overgrown with vegetation so its not clear whether the bee-eaters still breed but they still perch regularly on the wires.

15.   The Depuradora de S'Illot is the site birders mean when they talk about 'The Depuradora' even though Mallorca has many more of these water treatment plants. This one, although quite modern in construction, has a number of freshwater lagoons. Birds such as stilts and Shelducks breed here and good numbers of dabbling ducks are usually present amongst which there might be Marbled Duck. Birds such as Gull-billed Tern, Whiskered Tern and Collared Pratincole sometimes spend time here and in 2012 there was a pair of Black-necked Grebe too. Thankfully the site is overlooked by an observation platform which is also useful for scanning over a wider area in search of Marsh Harrier, herons and hirundines such as Red-rumped Swallow. To get there, turn right at the bus depot (see site 14) and continue for 1.8 km looking for a track to the left marked by a wooden 'binoculars' sign (39.7785N, 3.1199E). Follow this track, keeping right, until you reach a car park next to the platform (39.7757N, 3.1146E) after 500 metres.

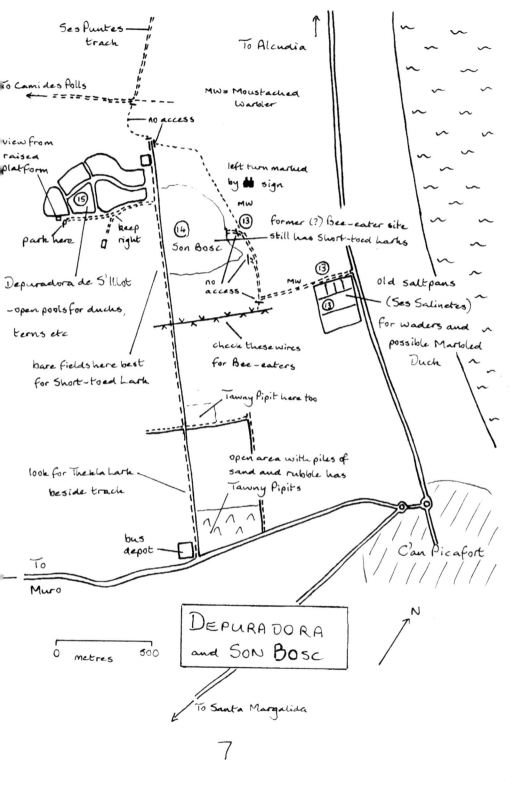

Tucan Marsh

A small wetland hemmed in by development but worth checking for passage terns and waders

Getting there

Between Alcudia old town and the Alcudia resort is a roundabout with Burger King on one side and a Lidl store on another. From this roundabout, head towards the old town but turn left down a track (39.8408N, 3.1214E) almost immediately after the Lidl store. The open water of the marsh is soon visible on either side of this track.

Notes

1. In spring, when the water levels are usually high, the main birds here are Coot, Moorhen Black-winged Stilt, Little Egret, Grey Heron and Cormorant but Little Grebe and Purple Swamphen also breed and there are usually a few other waders such as Common Sandpiper and Greenshank. Terns such as Whiskered and Gull-billed sometimes feed here and, especially if the water level falls, other passage waders may occur. Other species recorded here have included Purple Heron, Night Heron and Spotted Crake so it is always worth at least a brief look.

Son Real

This is reputed to be the best place in Mallorca for Dartford Warbler; Balearic Warbler breeds there too as well as Thekla Lark, Wryneck and Stone Curlew.

Getting there

From Alcudia, take the road towards Arta until, 3.2 km after the last roundabout in C'an Picafort, you see a track (39.7352N, 3.1807E) to Son Real on the left, signposted and marked by a number of flags. Follow this track to a car park next to Son Real farm. There are a number of trails leading to the coast from there.

Notes

2. This site was brought to the attention of birders by a recent book 'A Birding Tourist's Guide to Majorca', written by Mallorcan birders. Their description of the site begins 'There can be very few sites as outstanding as Son Real for seeing with relative ease the range of Majorcan Sylvia warblers' by which they mean Balearic and Dartford Warbler as well as Sardinian Warbler and Blackcap. Suitably enthused I visited the site in mid-April 2012 but, apart from getting hopelessly lost and soaking wet, was disappointed not to find either Balearic or Dartford Warbler. I subsequently spoke to lots of other birders that year and ALL those who had visited the site had also failed to find the two specialities. On the other hand, one contributor to the BirdForum pages said he'd been there 3 times and had Dartford Warbler each time. Of course the birds must be there but maybe April is a time when they are silent although one birder had failed in March too when they should have been at their noisiest. Bear in mind that you'll have to walk through almost 2 km of relatively unproductive pine forest before you reach open coastal scrub where these warblers might be found. One reputedly good spot is by a wooden observation platform (39.7526N, 3.1858E). Son Real may still be the best place on mainland Mallorca for Dartford Warbler but, at least in April, you should expect them to be difficult. Even if you don't find the specialities, other birds to enjoy include Thekla Lark in the coastal scrub, Wryneck and Crossbill in the pines and Stone Curlew and Red-legged Partridge in the walled fields. Pay attention to the various routes marked; I found it easy to follow the wrong one back from the coast.

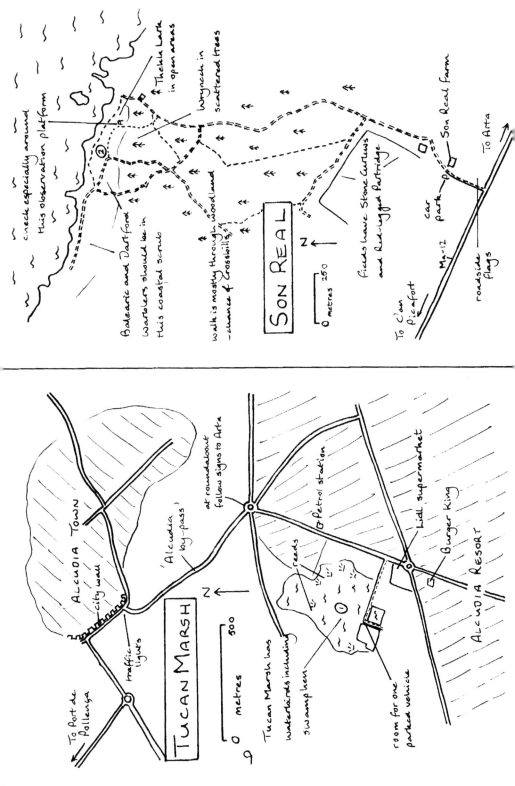

SON REAL

check especially around this observation platform

Thekla Lark in open areas

Wryneck in scattered trees

Balearic and Dartford Warblers should be in this coastal scrub

walk is mostly through woodland — chance of Crossbills?

N

0 metres 250

Fields have Stone Curlews and Red-legged Partridge

Son Real Farm

To Arta

To Can Picafort

Ma-12

car park

roadside flags

TUCAN MARSH

To Port de Pollença

ALCUDIA TOWN

city wall

traffic lights

'Alcudia by-pass'

at roundabout follow signs to Arta

Petrol station

reeds

Lidl supermarket

Burger King

ALCUDIA RESORT

room for one parked vehicle

Tucan Marsh has waterlands including swamphen

N

0 metres 500

Port de Pollença

Attraction

The perfect base for getting to Formentor, Albufereta, Albufera and the mountains and also a delightful place to stay (infinitely nicer than Alcudia) with some good birding within walking distance.

Getting there

From Palma take the Ma-13 via Inca and Pollença and you can be in Port de Pollença within 50 minutes.

Notes

1. From the south end of the town, two tracks, the Cami de Llenaire and the Cami de ca Volantina mark the beginning of an area known to birders as the 'Back Lanes' (see page 14) which provide enjoyable birdwatching walks.

2. There's a reliable site for Scops Owl close to the Pollensa Park hotel. From the beach road along the front of Pollença, turn inland, opposite the beach bar, along the road towards the Pollensa Park hotel but then turn almost immediately left opposite a Spar shop. This is a service road with the backs of the Pollentia and Uyal hotels on the left and the grounds of the Pollensa Park on the right. Follow this for 200 metres; the favoured spot for the owls is the last tree on the right at the end of the Pollensa Park grounds (39.8956N, 3.0777W). At dusk (around 9pm in late April) both the male and female would sit in this tree or on the nearby poles and wires or on window ledges at the backs of the hotels.

3. Audouin's Gull used to be erratic in its occurrences around Pollença Bay but now it's easy to get really close views of them on the beach. They're only present in small numbers but they will stand right next to sunbathers hoping for a few scraps. A few Yellow-legged Gulls may be present too. Just off the beach are a couple of breakwaters and these provide resting places for groups of Shags and maybe the odd Sandwich Tern too.

4. Another popular spot for looking for Scops Owl is in front of the Guardia Civil building at the back of a small park with a play area. Stand in the car park in front of the building at 9 pm (in late April) and listen for their calls.

5. The Zona de Humida la Gola (or just La Gola) is a small local nature reserve within the town. It comprises a series of short trails around a shallow pool (39.9025N, 3.0793W) and streams and through areas of scrub and pine wood. Birds such as Mallard, Little Egret, Black-winged Stilt and Yellow-legged Gull are usually present plus a few waders such as Common Sandpiper and occasionally other herons such as Grey, Squacco and Night. It becomes much more attractive to birds if the water levels fall and it makes a decent little wader pool. Crossbills are often present in the pines and the various bushes may hold migrants such as chats and warblers. Hirundines often fly over the pool and Ospreys have been seen to catch fish here. The site is easily accessed via the lanes behind Tolo's or Torre Playa restaurants. An information hut (39.9029N, 3.0793W) has been built but was closed in 2012.

6. There's a good spot for Stone Curlews in a field (39.9075N, 3.0763W) to the left of the by-pass as you drive towards Formentor from the main roundabout in Port de Pollença (the one with the sculpture of a seaplane).

7. The best birding within walking distance of Pollença is in and around the Boquer Valley (see over)

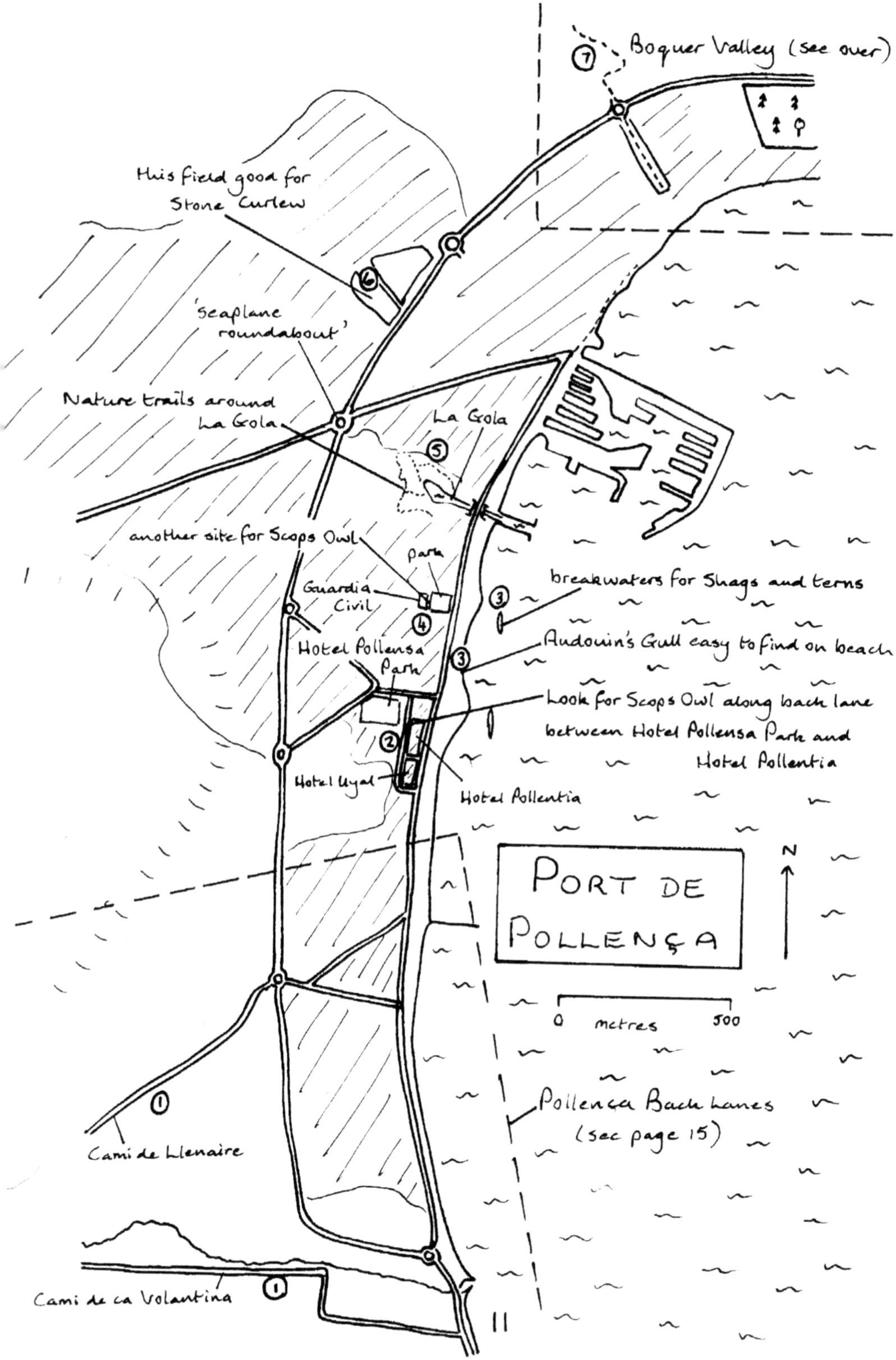

⑦ Boquer Valley (see over)

This field good for
Stone Curlew

⑥

'seaplane
roundabout'

Nature trails around
La Gola

La Gola

⑤

another site for Scops Owl

Park

Guardia
Civil

④

breakwaters for Shags and terns

③

Audouin's Gull easy to find on beach

Hotel Pollensa
Park

③

Look for Scops Owl along back lane
between Hotel Pollensa Park and
Hotel Pollentia

②

Hotel Uyal

Hotel Pollentia

PORT DE
POLLENÇA

N

0   metres   500

Pollença Back Lanes
(see page 15)

① Cami de Llenaire

① Cami de ca Volantina

11

Boquer Valley

Attraction

The valley itself has breeding Booted Eagle, Blue Rock Thrush, Crag Martin, Cirl Bunting and even Balearic Warbler. There's always a chance of raptors overhead including Peregrine, Eleonora's Falcon and Black Vulture. At the base of the valley are several spots that are worth checking for migrants.

Getting there

From the 'seaplane roundabout' in Port de Pollença, take the by-pass towards Formentor and turn left at the second roundabout to reach a small car park (39.9130N, 3.0841E).

Access

The path into the Boquer Valley passes through a gate to a farm (the Casa de Boquer) and there have been fears that the public might be denied access through this gate. However, by 2012, the path was prominently signposed (Cami de Cala Boquer) and was being used by so many people that it seems to be an institution. Surely they couldn't close it now?

Notes

1. The area between the car park and the farm has long been a favoured spot for looking for migrants, especially flycatchers and redstarts but the olive and fig groves seem to have deteriorated and these birds are now fewer in number. You might see more birds by walking back along the by-pass and checking the field and its fig trees to your right; in 2012 we had Stone Curlew, Wryneck and Whitethroat here as well as the usual flycatchers and redstarts.

2. Where the path passes the farmhouse there's a good vantage point over the surrounding fields. You might see Cirl Bunting, Stone Curlew or a migrant Golden Oriole in and around these fields but in 2012 the highlight was the fantastic views of a pair of Booted Eagles, one of two pairs in the valley.

3. Beyond the farmhouse, the path passes between two tall rocks. This is a good site for Blue Rock Thrush and Crag Martin as well as the usual Sardinian Warblers etc.

4. Beyond the stand of pines on the left, the path passes through a gap in a wall. Just before this is a little culvert to the right which marks the location of a little spring (approx 39.9211N, 3.0872E). Birds such as Sardinian Warbler and Stonechat plus migrant warblers etc come down to this water. In 2012 there were several reports of a pair of Bonelli's Eagle over the valley; a few have been released on the island hoping to get them breeding here again.

5. Balearic Warbler presumably still breeds in the valley but in April 2012 I couldn't find any. The best bet is in the areas that become visible when the sea comes into view.

6. Perhaps the best place for migrants is along 'Pine Tree Avenue' on the coastal side of the Boquer roundabout. Don't forget to check here for warblers, flycatchers, chats, wheatears and redstarts; it's easier to see these birds in the tamarisks here than in the olives at site 1. Look out for Hoopoe on the grassy areas below the trees.

7. The Bosque de Pollença is known to birders as Postage Stamp Wood because of its shape. It has potential for migrants (I've had Bonelli's Warbler and Subalpine Warbler there in the past) but is often disappointing. The scrub between here and the car park might have a few birds such as warblers and Woodchat Shrike

BOQUER VALLEY

0 metres 250

N

Balearic Warbler more likely from here onwards ⑤

⑤

⑤

Booted Eagle regular over valley

wall

gap

④

small spring may attract birds to drink and bathe

stand of pines

look for Blue Rock Thrush, Crag Martin etc around these two tall rocks

③

Casade Boquer

scan from here ②

check olive groves for migrants

①

car park

walk along here to check fields and fig trees

⑥

Postage Stamp Wood best bet for wood-loving migrants such as Bonelli's Warbler

⑦

pine tree avenue now best for migrants

still a chance of migrants in this scrub

Pollença Back Lanes

Attraction

It's easy to walk or cycle to this attractive area from Port de Pollença. A mixture of farmland, streams, pools and orchards provide a variety of habitats for migrants as well as breeding birds making this a good place to look for birds such as Bee-eater, Golden Oriole and Red-footed Falcon. It is one of the most reliable places on the island for both Spotless Starling and Tree Sparrow.

Getting there

From Port de Pollença look for the Cami de Llenaire (off one of the roundabouts of the bypass) or the Cami de Ca Volantina (next right along the coast road after the last roundabout).

Notes

1.   The Cami de Llenaire road passes through a couple of fig groves (eg either side of the track to the Hotel Llenaire) in which both Wryneck and Golden Oriole have been regularly seen though both can be elusive. Check the sparrow flocks for Tree Sparrow.

2.   The Cami de Ca Volantina road passes alongside the Torrent de San Jordi stream. This is worth checking for waders; as well as the breeding Little Ringed Plovers and Common Sandpipers I had Snipe, Greenshank, Green Sandpiper and Stone Curlew. It looks like the sort of place where someone might one day find a crake or two. Other birds here included Serin, Nightingale, Cetti's Warbler, Sardinian Warbler, Corn Bunting, flava Wagtail and, on one visit, a Water Pipit. Further up the road is another fig grove for flycatchers, redstarts, Woodchat Shrike and, perhaps, Wryneck and Golden Oriole.

3.   Opposite where the Cami de Ca Volantina meets the Cami de Llenaire is an open area with wires overhead. This spot used to be called The Beehives and, although the hives have gone, there's still a chance of Bee-eaters here either flying around or perching on the wires.

4.   Another productive stream is the site known as 'smelly river'. Here again you'll find species such as Common Sandpiper, Nightingale and Cetti's Warbler and in the evening there's a chance of seeing Night Herons coming from their roost. On the opposite side of the road, the wooded hillside is worth scanning over for Eleonora's Falcon (eg for some reason 8 birds flew around this hillside for a whole day on 7th May 1991).

5.-   The C'an Cuarassa track has been managed to provide viewing screens overlooking some small wader pools. Park near the C'an Cuarassa restaurant (39.8779N, 3.0818E) and follow the track, parallel to the main road, through a gate until the screens come into view on the right. There are two pools that have been screened and the birds likely to be seen from the 'hides' include stilts, Common Sandpipers, Greenshanks and Redshanks. However, at least in spring, an even better pool is on the left (from 39.8751N, 3.0824E), opposite the first screen. Birds seen here in April 2012 included Grey Plover, Sanderling, Kentish, Ringed and Little Ringed Plovers, Redshank, Greenshank and Green Sandpiper. This track is also a good place to look for Bluethroat in winter and you should check the many wires within view for birds such as Roller and, especially in May, Red-footed Falcon.

6.   Another branch of the C'an Cuarassa track heads directly inland (from 39.8769N, 3.0812E). The open areas here are particularly good for pipits (Red-throated has been seen), wagtails (I had at least 40 flava wagtails on one visit) and chats and this is the best place on the island for Spotless Starling. I also had a Great White Egret by this track in 2012.

PORT DE POLLENÇA
(see page 11)

Cami de Llenaire

check fig groves for
orioles and wrynecks

Hotel Llenaire

check here for
Bee-eaters

③

① ① ①

② ②

park
here

Torrent de
Sant Jordi

Cami de ca Volantina

stream surprisingly
good for waders

Club del Sol

C'an
Cuarrassa
restaurant

'smelly stream'
for waders, herons
and warblers

best area for
Spotless Starling

⑥ ⑥

open fields for pipits
wagtails, chats and
Falcons

shallow pools
for waders
in spring

④

⑤ ⑤

④

look for Eleonora's
over this hill in early May

screened pools for
waders

⑤

POLLENÇA
BACK LANES

0 metres 500

N

Albufereta
(see over)

15

Albufereta

Attraction

Smaller than S'Albufera and more difficult to access but this is a great place for waterbirds including Osprey, Marsh Harrier, Purple Swamphen and a variety of herons that now includes a few almost unmissable Great White Egrets. Migrant terns are often seen over the water and Eleonora's Falcons hunt here at dawn and dusk at least in May.

Getting there

Located inland from the coastal road between Port de Pollença and Alcudia. There are access points from this road and also from the lanes along its western side.

Notes

1. The most popular viewing point for the reserve is the 'raised mound'. There are pools on either side of this spot and from here you should nowadays see Great White Egret and Red-crested Pochard at least. Scan the edges for Purple Swamphen, Squacco Heron and Purple Heron and look for terns such as Whiskered or Gull-billed over the water. To reach this place, look for a slip road (39.8586N, 3.1000E) behind some green and white bollards immediately south of where the coastal road crosses the Torrent de Albufereta. Park at the end of this slip road and walk inland along the track towards a copse of pines. This track ends at a private finca but there is a path to the right through the pines. This joins with a walled path that takes you behind the finca to the 'raised mound'(39.8552N, 3.0976E). There's a chance of migrants such as chats, wagtails and pipits all around here and we had a Siberian Chiffchaff near the parking area in April 2012. Look out too for Stone Curlews, eg in the fields around the finca or by the derelict building to the north.

2. There is now a hide overlooking some of the reserve. Sadly, it overlooks a pool which isn't particularly productive but it does offer an elevated viewpoint for scanning over the rest of the marsh for herons, Marsh Harriers etc. To reach the hide, park on the lane down the south side of the Club Pollentia and walk around the back of this resort. Follow the path into the resort itself until you see a path to the left leading out to the hide (39.8628N, 3.0912E) in the marsh. I've had Bluethroat in this area in the past.

3. It is possible to get close to the marsh by walking down the track (39.8577N, 3.0797E) opposite the Villa Lorenzo (just south of an abandoned windmill). This can be good for Stone Curlews and migrant chats etc but is too low to offer views of the reserve.

4. For a more elevated view, continue south along the back road for a further 450 metres until it rises slightly over a small hill. At the crest of this hill there's a track to the left (39.8546N, 3.0829E) just before a fenced orchard. A short walk down this track gives you good views over the reserve for herons, harriers, terns and ducks.

5. The easiest viewpoint over the reserve is found by continuing along the back road for a further 1.1 km until, just before some wires cross the road, there is a tiny pull in on the left (39.8504N, 3.0931E). Scan from here for herons, terns and harriers and see how many ducks and Great White Egrets you can count. Look back along the overhead wires for Ospreys sitting on the pylons and check the wires too for Red-footed Falcons or Rollers. In 2012, a pair of Stone Curlews was nesting in one of the fields here.

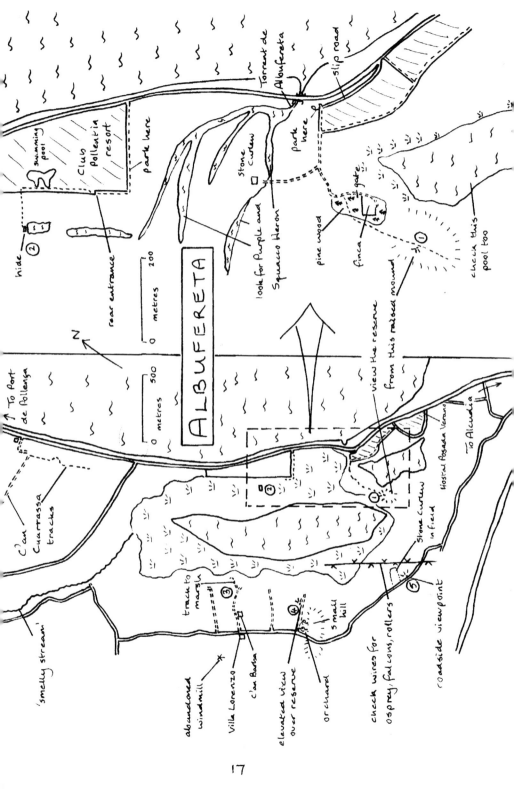

ALBUFERETA

Torrent de Albufereta

slip road

park here

Club Pollentia resort

Swimming pool

rear entrance

park here

hide ②

look for Purple and Squacco Heron

Stone Curlew

pine wood

gate

finca

①

check this pool too

N

To Port de Pollença

metres 500 0

metres 200 0

view the reserve from this raised mound

C'an Cuarrassa tracks

'smelly stream'

abandoned windmill

track to marsh ③

Villa Lorenzo

C'an Barba

②

①

elevated view over reserve

orchard

Stone Curlew in field

check wires for osprey, falcons, rollers

④

's mall hill

⑤

roadside viewpoint

Hostal Posada Verano

To Alcudia

17

Cape Formentor

Attraction

Most famous as a breeding site for dozens of pairs of Eleonora's Falcons but is also good for seawatching (Cory's and Balearic Shearwater are easily seen), raptor passage and migrant passerines. Balearic Warbler also breeds here.

Getting there

There is just one road along the peninsula, easily found by following signs to Formentor from Port de Pollença.

Notes

1. At the top of the first hill out of Pollença is a mirador with a large car park on the left and, usually, swarms of tourists. This is one of several viewpoints for looking for Eleonora's Falcon and, when it's not too busy, there's a chance of Blue Rock Thrush and Balearic Warbler.

2. Opposite the car park at site 1, a road winds up to the right, passing more habitat for Blue Rock Thrush and Balearic Warbler, until it terminates just below a tower, the Talaia de Albercutx (39.9274N, 3.1146E). It's possible to scramble up to the tower itself and from there you get a panoramic view over the Formentor peninsula, Pollença Bay and back towards the Tramuntana mountains. This perfect vantage point makes this the best place on the island for watching for passing raptors. Birds such as Buzzard (in April), Marsh Harrier and Honey Buzzard (in May) sometimes reach double figures in a day and there are regular sightings of Booted Eagle, Red Kite, Osprey, Peregrine and, of course, Eleonora's Falcon. During the course of a season, Short-toed Eagle, Bonelli's Eagle, Egyptian Vulture Hobby, Red-footed Falcon, Montagu's Harrier, Black Kite, Alpine Swift and Black Stork are also likely to be seen. Rarities have included Pallid Harrier and Rough-legged Buzzard.

3. Cases Velles (or Casas Veyas) is said to be the best place for migrant passerines on mainland Mallorca. It pulls in migrants because it is the first (or last) area of cultivation on the Formentor peninsula, including two fields of fig trees. Sadly however, access to this area has been blocked by fences and no entry signs, so the site can only be viewed by peering through the fences from the roadside. Even so, at passage times, you can see birds like redstarts, flycatchers, whinchats, wheatears and Woodchat Shrikes and this is one of the best spots for finding Ortolan Bunting. However, given the limited access, stops here are often a little disappointing. The nearby pine woods have lots of Crossbills and Firecrests. The fig fields are obvious from the roadside (39.9433N, 3.1524E) just after km 11.(In 2010, Hilary MacBean reported that she managed to walk to the fig fields by finding a path from the car park at km 13. However, the only paths we found in 2012 were blocked by more fences.)

4. From the car park at km 13 there is a well-marked path (Cami de Murtes) which takes you into the pine forests. It won't be long before you've at least heard Firecrests and Crossbills. We had better views of the Crossbills (of the large-billed Mallorcan race) by waiting for them to drink at a temporary puddle in the car park (39.9488N, 3.1715E). There's another promising puddle by the roadside at km 12.25 which still had water in May when the other one had dried up.

5. In my experience, the best mirador for watching Eleonora's Falcon is to the left of the road at km 16.8 (39.9555N, 3.2008E). By mid-May they are numerous along this coast but when they first arrive, in late April, this is the best location to try. I had a singing Balearic Warbler here too.

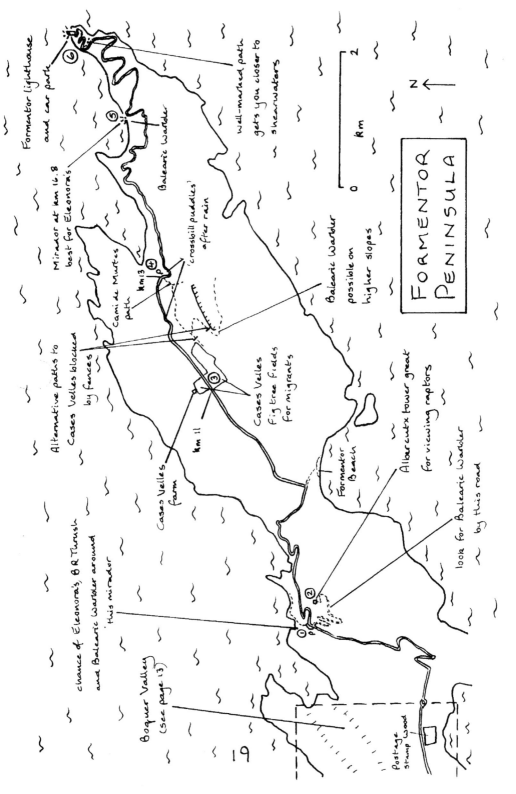

FORMENTOR PENINSULA

Formentor lighthouse and car park

⑥

⑤

Mirador at km 16.8 best for Eleonora's

Camí de Muntes path

km 13 ⊕

'crossbill puddles' after rain

Well-marked path gets you closer to shearwaters

(Balearic Warbler)

Balearic Warbler possible on higher slopes

Alternative paths to Cases Velles blocked by fences

Cases Velles Fig tree Fields for migrants

km 11

Cases Velles Farm

③

chance of Eleonora's, BR Thrush and Balearic Warbler around this mirador

Boquer Valley (see page 13)

Formentor Beach

② Albercutx tower great for viewing raptors

① look for Balearic Warbler by this road

Postage Stamp Wood

N ←

0   km   2

19

6. Formentor lighthouse at the tip of the peninsula provides another clifftop viewpoint for looking for falcons and also seabirds. This is one of the best places for seeing Cory's and Balearic Shearwater but the views are rather distant and the car park is usually crowded and best avoided. Instead, try to find a pull-in further back along the road and look for the well-marked rocky path (from 39.9606N, 3.2112E) down towards the sea on the east side of the peninsula. This path with steps and fences gets you to a lower vantage point from which you can get closer to the shearwaters. The light gets better later in the day.

The Central Plain

Attraction

If you drive from north to south through Mallorca you will pass through areas of low-lying farmland that can be good for birds in their own right. This area has high densities of Quail, Stone Curlew, Red-legged Partridge and Short-toed Lark and Thekla Lark is widespread. But the main attraction is during passage times when birds such as Red-footed falcon and Lesser Kestrel may be present in small parties.

Getting there

En route between north and south it's well worth making a detour. The areas around Vilafranca de Bonany and Maria de la Salut are found to the west of the MA-3340 road that connects Santa Margalida and Petra.

Notes

1. The area just north of Maria de la Salut is one of the best for passage falcons. Up to 6 Lesser Kestrels were present in May 2010 and again in 2011 for most of April with smaller numbers in May and July too. At times they could be seen alongside Red-footed Falcons: 2 in May 2010 and 6 in May 2011. The area is particularly good for larks; apart from the common Short-toed Larks and less common Thekla Larks, 4 Calandra Larks were seen here in April 2011 and the pipits seen here have included Red-throated. The best way to find the falcons is to drive slowly along the roads to the north of town. The road to Muro is especially promising as it is crossed by 3 sets of overhead wires (eg 39.6860N, 3.0611E) on which these birds often sit.

2. Another good area for falcons is around Vilafranca de Bonany; there were 12 Red-footed Falcons here in late May 2011. This area also gets regular sightings of Short-toed Eagle and in the winter of 2011-12 an Italian Sparrow was also present.

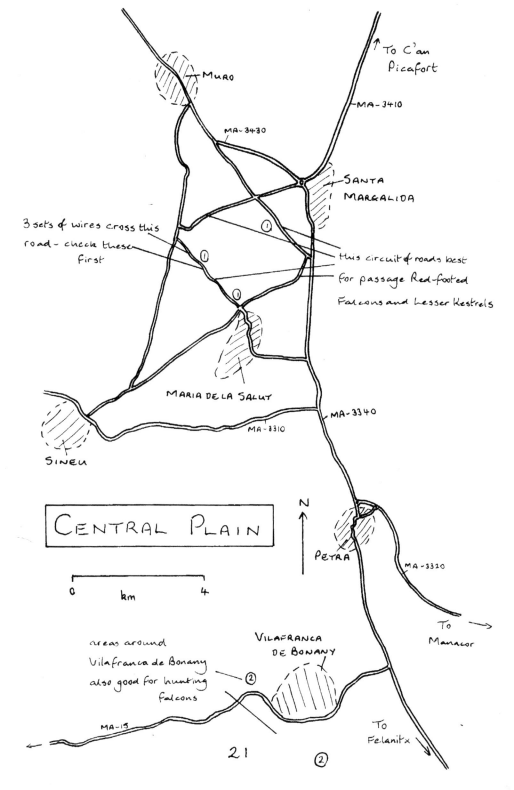

To C'an Picafort

MA-3410

MURO

MA-3430

SANTA MARGALIDA

3 sets of wires cross this road - check these first

this circuit of roads best for passage Red-footed Falcons and Lesser Kestrels

MARIA DE LA SALUT

MA-3340

MA-3310

SINEU

CENTRAL PLAIN

N

0 km 4

PETRA

MA-3320

To Manacor

areas around Vilafranca de Bonany also good for hunting falcons

②

VILAFRANCA DE BONANY

MA-15

21

②

To Felanitx

The Arta mountains and Betlem

Attraction

Somewhere in the Arta mountains is the only pair of Egyptian Vultures remaining on Mallorca. There are also breeding Thekla Larks and Balearic Warblers and good places to look for migrant passerines and passing seabirds.

Getting there

Arta is well-signposted from Alcudia.

Notes

1. The road to Ermita de Betlem passes a radio mast near its highest point. Park in the next lay-by on the right (39.7322N, 3.3189E) and walk behind the mast to overlook a small valley. Alternatively, look for a track to the left 160 metres further along the road. You can walk along here to a tiny reservoir (often dry) via more good habitat. You should see birds such as Thekla Lark, Raven, Tawny Pipit and Booted Eagle and the valley can sometimes be good for migrants. This area has had Red-billed Chough and Alpine Accentor outside the breeding season and Rock Thrush on passage.

2. Cap Capdepera is the most easterly site on Mallorca and hence offers great potential as a seawatching site. You should at least see Cory's and Balearic Shearwaters. It can be reached by taking the Cala Ratjada road through Arta and continuing to the headland (39.7156N, 3.4769E) beyond the resort.

3. A good spot for migrants and breeding Balearic Warblers is found by walking the coastal track (Cami des Calo) from the urbanisation of Betlem. To get there, take the road towards Arta but look for a left turn to Colonia Sant Pere. Follow this road as far as you can until, just beyond the urbanisation of Betlem (39.7554N, 3.3220E), it degenerates and becomes too rough for many vehicles. From there you can follow the track on foot for almost 3 km to the headland of Es Calo. I visited here on 22nd April when, in a strong northerly wind, dozens of warblers (Blackcaps, phylloscs and Whitethroats) were pouring south (yes, south). That morning marked the first obvious arrival of migrants including Pied and Spotted Flycatchers. I had a Bonelli's Warbler in the plantation by the parking area and a Wryneck in the pines to the left of the path further on. The habitat is good for Balearic Warbler; they do breed here but wouldn't show for us in those winds.

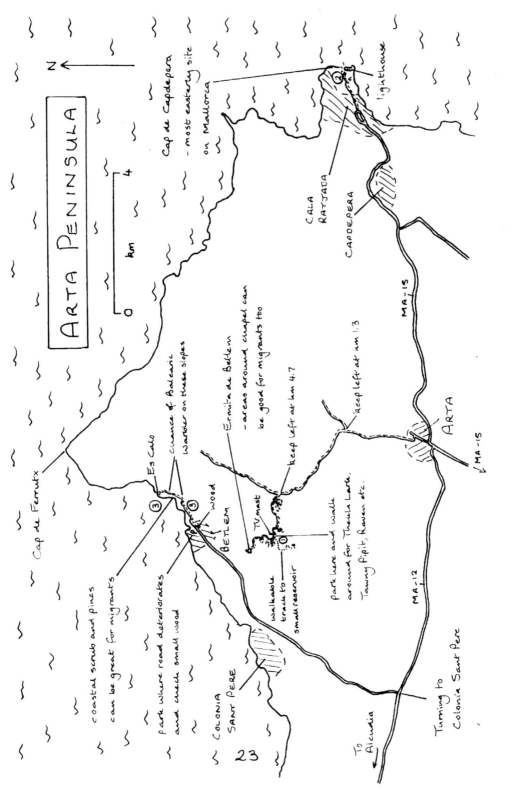

ARTA PENINSULA

N ←

0 — 4 km

Cap de Capdepera
– most easterly site
on Mallorca

Lighthouse

CALA RATJADA

CAPDEPERA

MA-15

Cap de Ferrutx

coastal scrub and pines
can be great for migrants

park where road deteriorates
and check small wood

Es Cula

chance of Balearic
Warbler on these slopes

Ermita de Bellem
– areas around chapel can
be good for migrants too

keep left at km 4.7

keep left at km 1.3

ARTA

MA-15

wood

BETLEM

③   ③

TV mast

①

walkable track to
small reservoir

park here and walk
around for Thekla Lark,
Tawny Pipit, Raven etc.

MA-12

COLONIA
SANT PERE

To Alcudia

Turning to
Colonia Sant Pere

23

Tramuntana mountains

Attraction

This range of mountains across the north and west side of the island is particularly good for raptors including Black Vulture, Booted Eagle, Red Kite, Eleonora's Falcon and, now, Griffon Vulture too. Other breeding birds include Spectacled Warbler, Rock Thrush and Moltoni's Subalpine Warbler.

Getting there

From Pollença follow signs to Soller. It's best to set off before 8.30 am, at least in April, to avoid the hundreds of cyclists who also use this route

Notes

1. The Ternelles Valley offers a chance of birds such as Blue Rock Thrush and raptors overhead such as Black Vulture, Eleonora's Falcon and Booted Eagle. However access is limited to certain days (in the past it has been Saturdays only) and even then it is necessary to get a permit (ask at the tourist office in Port de Pollença). Although there's a pleasant walk for about 5km, all the way to the Castell del Rei perched above the seacliffs, you're only likely to see the species you can see in the Boquer Valley anyway. The entrance to the Ternelles valley (39.8831N, 3.0138E) is off the road to Soller, opposite the Roman bridge by the village of Pollença.

2. Another walk from the mountain road towards the coast can be done at Mortitx. This has no access restrictions and offers a better chance of finding Balearic Warbler too. Apparently in winter this area can be good for finches such as Siskin, Brambling and Hawfinch that are otherwise rare in Mallorca. The entrance to this walk (39.8679N, 2.9245E) is clearly signed to Mortitx just before km 11 on the mountain road. There's a detailed map of this walk at www.birdguides.com/i/prods/BKMupdatemap.jpg.

3. One of the best ways to see Black Vultures at closer range is to climb Mount Tomir, the third highest mountain in Mallorca (1,104 metres). There's also a chance of Alpine Accentor up here in winter until the end of March at least. To get there, turn inland at km 17.4 on a gated road (39.8300N, 2.8965E) signposted to Manut Binifaldo. You can follow this for 3 km to a bottling plant and walk from there but it's at least a 2 hour walk to the summit.

4. Lluc monastery is a popular tourist attraction in its own right but from a birding point of view, the open areas here give you a chance to scan for Booted Eagle and Black Vulture (both likely during a visit) and the parkland around the monastery has breeding Firecrests. However, the highlight on my visit were the calling Wrynecks in and around the car park. I heard them from all 4 corners of the parking area but only heard 2 birds at any one time.

5. If you are lucky you can get fantastic views of Black Vulture and Booted Eagle from the mirador at km 12.5 (39.8287N, 2.8371E) overlooking the Torrent de Pareis. In July 2012 Steve Hearn had over 35 Eleonora's Falcons from here.

6. The walk around Cuber Reservoir offers a chance of all the mountain birds including, potentially, 10 species of raptor and the scarce but difficult passerines such as Spectacled Warbler, Moltoni's Subalpine Warbler and Rock Thrush (see over)

7. The walk to the summit of Puig de L'Ofre can be productive. In July 2012 Steve Hearn had 3 Eleonora's, 3 Griffons, close views of 3 Black Vultures (at eye level at the summit) and a male Rock Thrush near the first telescope overlooking Soller.

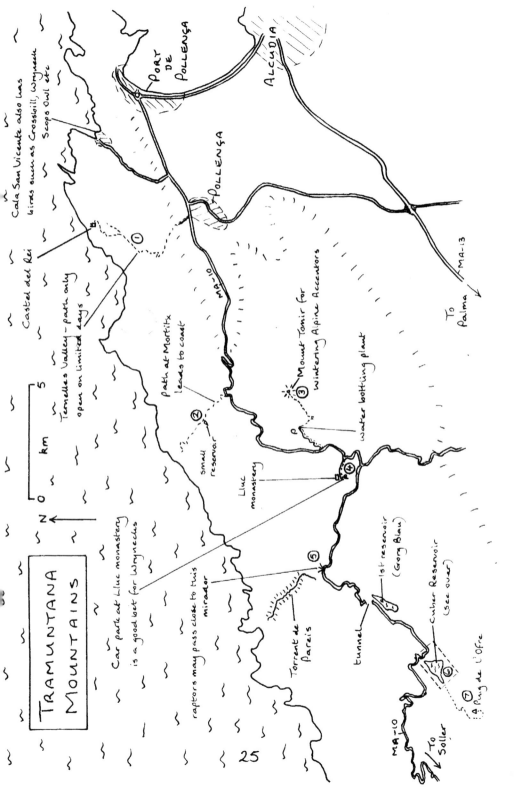

TRAMUNTANA MOUNTAINS

N ←

0   km   5

Cala San Vicente also has birds such as Crossbill, Wryneck, Scops Owl etc

Castel del Rei

Ternelles Valley — path only open on limited days

①

Port de Pollença

Alcudia

Pollença

MA-10

Path at Mortitx leads to coast

To Palma

MA-13

② small reservoir

③ Mount Tomir for wintering Alpine Accentors

water bottling plant

Lluc monastery

Car park at Lluc monastery is a good lost for Wrynecks

raptors may pass close to this mirador

⑤

Torrent de Pareis

tunnel

1st reservoir (Gorg Blau)

Cuber Reservoir (see over)

⑥ Puig de l'Ofre

⑦

MA-10

To Soller

25

Cuber Reservoir

Attraction

This is probably the best place on Mallorca to see three difficult passerines, (Rufous-tailed) Rock Thrush, Spectacled Warbler and Moltoni's Subalpine Warbler. Even if these difficult species prove elusive you will at least see a variety of birds of prey including Black Vulture.

Getting there

The reservoir comes into view as you reach the car park (39.7872N, 2.7969E) at km 34. In fact there's a choice of 3 car parks here, so park where you can and walk around the reservoir.

Notes

1. The open area to the right of where the track begins often has a pair of Tawny Pipits. There's also a chance of Cirl Bunting and there has been at least one report of Rock Thrush here.

2. Before you reach the dam, the track passes through open grassy areas with scattered pines on the left. This used to be a reliable site for Spectacled Warbler but the pines have grown up making the habitat less suitable. However, although most people miss them (including me in 3 visits in 2012), there are sightings in most years either just before the dam (on either side of the path) or maybe just below the dam. If you miss the Spectacled Warbler there is still a chance of another, potentially greater, prize. The Subalpine Warbler which breeds on Corsica, Sardinia and Mallorca is of the race moltoni which has more subdued plumage tones, a less distinct white 'moustache' and an utterly different call – a loud Wren-like 'trrrt'. It has now been found in parts of Italy too and, since it doesn't interbreed with birds of the nominate race, it has been suggested that it should be treated as a separate species, Moltoni's Warbler. In Mallorca it breeds sparsely in the Tramuntana mountains and the best known site for it is here at Cuber. Even so, I failed to find one in 2 visits in late April 2012 but then on 3rd May, found a male calling and song-flighting (only briefly) in these pines to the left of the path. They apparently arrive relatively late in April, compared to the nominate race birds that pass through, so maybe this bird had only just arrived.

3. In 2012 I concentrated my search for Moltoni's and Spectacled Warblers in the little valley below the dam as this is where both species have been found in the past. However, I only had birds such as Cirl Bunting, Nightingale, Blackcap and Pied and Spotted Flycatchers. Raptors can be seen in the skies from any point around the reservoir. Black Vulture and Booted Eagle are pretty much guaranteed, albeit often distantly, and most diligent birders now see Red Kite and Griffon Vulture too. There are frequent sightings of Kestrel, Peregrine, Osprey and Eleonora's Falcon. If migrants such as Montagu's Harrier, Egyptian Vulture or Short-toed Eagle are also seen, 10 raptors in a day is possible. The Griffon Vultures are a recent phenomenon; there was an influx of dozens of these birds in 2009 and by 2012 at least one pair was breeding on the island. Scanning for raptors is made more problematic by the hundreds of Yellow-legged Gulls that rest on the reservoir and are constantly in the air.

4. The best-known site for (Rufous-tailed) Rock Thrush is in the quarry just past the dam. Although they have bred here in the past, most birders fail to see them nowadays. What reports there are tend to be of birds further up the mountain paths, from May onwards. I had a Blue Rock Thrush at the quarry on the first of my 3 visits in 2012.

5. Graham Hearl's book suggests that the north-west side of the dam is also good for breeding Subalpine Warbler but I couldn't find any in 2012, just species such as Firecrest, Nightingale, Blackcap and Little Ringed Plover.

Cuber Reservoir

N ↑

0 metres 250

keep scanning for Black Vulture
Booted Eagle, Griffon Vulture, Red Kite,
Peregrine, Osprey and Eleonora's

no sign of Moltoni's Warbler in 2012

To Soller

no access to this valley

park where you can

P

P

To Pollensa

Helipad
H

① pines had Moltoni's Subalpine Warbler in 2012

② formerly best area for Spectacled Warbler now overgrown with pines

causeway

open area for Tawny Pipit

Cuber Reservoir

100's Yellow-legged Gulls rest on reservoir

Cirl Bunting on slopes

Rock Thrush possible anywhere on this hillside including the quarry

Valley below dam has been good for Moltoni's Warbler

To Puig de l'Ofre

27

Palma to Port de Soller

Attraction

Red Kites are probably more numerous in this part of the island and there are plenty of Booted Eagles too. One of the best places to see these birds is at the municipal dump at Son Reus. Another speciality is Alpine Accentor, a regular visitor to the castle at Alaro.

Getting there

From Palma, the MA-11 takes you to Port de Soller via Bunyola and Soller and the MA-13 towards Inca has a turn off north to Alaro. There is a tunnel on the MA-11 but you'll see more raptors by taking the more scenic 'old' route.

Notes

1. Just north of Palma airport is a small reservoir the Bassa de Can Guidet, also known as the Bassa de Son Ferriol, that is great for wildfowl in winter. Amongst the hundreds of Mallard and Little Grebe there are usually smaller numbers of birds such as Shoveler, Wigeon, Pochard and, more interestingly, Black-necked Grebes (sometimes in double figures). To get there from the airport take the ring road around the east side of Palma, following signs to Inca until, just past Son Ferriol, you see a turn off to Sineu (the MA-3011). Follow this for 3.5 km until, 1 km after s'Hostalot, you see a long straight paved road to the right (39.5874N, 2.7490E). The reservoir is on the left, 600 metres down this road.

2. Red Kites and, often, Booted Eagles can be seen at close range scavenging around the municipal dump at Son Reus. This site covers a large area, making quite a scar on the landscape but in 2012 I got closest to the birds as follows: from Palma, take the MA-11 towards Soller until, about 5 km after leaving the Palma ring road, you take a right turn signposted to Son Reus. Follow this for 500 metres then turn left following signs to an animal refuge. After a kilometre you reach a massive incinerator plant but immediately before this is a track to the right (39.6447N, 2.6787E) which leads to some gatehouses at the end of the complex. Beyond there are two raised hills in which the dumps are concealed, one to the left, one to the right. In late afternoon the site was unoccupied and we drove up onto the right hand hill where dozens of Yellow-legged Gulls were sitting around, up to 4 Red Kites were swooping for scraps and at least 3 Booted Eagles were flying around. On BirdForum, Alf King has also reported up to 5 Black Kites here in September.

3. In November 2010, Hilary MacBean reported getting great views of Balearic Shearwaters following boats into the harbour at Port de Soller each evening. She said they could be seen from cliffs overlooking the harbour but we struggled to find a decent vantage point on our visit. One possible viewpoint might be from or near the Nautica Bar (39.8010N, 2.6941W) on the Calle Belgica to the north of the harbour.

4. The Castell d'Alaro is set spectacularly in mountainous habitat giving an excellent chance of seeing Booted Eagles. The area is also noted for its wintering Alpine Accentors, though they can be elusive. To get there, take the Alaro turn off from the M-13 motorway then follow signs to the castell from Alaro village. This takes you up a winding road for almost 4 km to a car park at the restaurant of Es Verger (39.7291N, 2.7882E). There are then two routes to the castle on foot, the shortest of which is a walk of about 800m.

scan for shearwaters from here

③

Ma10 mountain road to Pollenca

PORT DE SOLLER

Cuber Reservoir (see page 27)

SOLLER

Castel Alaro for wintering Alpine Accentor

ORIENT

good area for raptors esp Booted Eagle

④

tunnel

look for raptors from old Soller road

Drive as far as Es Verger restaurant

+ ALARO

PALMA TO PORT DE SOLLER

BUNYOLA

N

0 km 4

MARATXI

incinerator plant

Son Reus dump attracts kites and Booted Eagles

Ma-13 main motorway to Pollenca

②

turn off signed to Son Reus

we drove onto this raised hill

roundabout

Bassa de Can Guidet gets hundreds of wildfowl in winter

Ma3013

s'Hostalot

To Sineu

PALMA

SON FERRIOL

Ma 3011

①

Ma 15 to Manacor

29

airport

Southern Mallorca

Attraction

Birders staying in the north of the island should make at least one excursion to the southern corner which has one of Mallorca's best wetlands (the Salobrar de Campos), possibly the best seawatching spot on the island (Cap de Ses Salines) and a number of sites for species such as Balearic Warbler (in my experience easier to find here than further north).

Getting there

From Palma or Alcudia follow roads via Santa Margalida and Petra to Felanitx. From there you can go west to Colonia San Jordi via Campos or east to Porto Colom or south to Ses Salines.

Notes

1. Cap Blanc (Cabo Blanco) has expansive areas of relatively undisturbed garrigue habitat and is therefore a productive area for species such as Thekla Lark, Tawny Pipit Stone Curlew and Balearic Warbler. It is possible to walk along the top of the cliffs for several kilometres west from the lighthouse but, carrying my camera gear I only managed to get as far as the nearest ruined bunkers. Even so I did find Wryneck, Woodchat Shrike and all the species listed above including a pair of Balearic Warblers visiting a nest site. To get there follow the road which runs about 4 km inland, west from the Salobrar de Campos. Ignore all turn offs and continue towards S'Arenal until you see a left turn signposted to Cabo Blanco. This short road ends at the gates (39.3659N, 2.7905E) to the lighthouse. There is room to park but there were many signs of smashed windows here so beware of thieves. There is a path down the right hand side of the drive to the lighthouse and you can explore westwards from there.

2. The extensive saltpans at Salobrar de Campos (formerly known as the Salinas de Levante) are fantastic for waterbirds including waders, herons, flamingos and, in winter, cranes (see page 34).

3   Colonia San Jordi is the departure point for boats to Cabrera (see page 32) but it also has a smaller set of saltpans, the Salinas de s'Avall which has a selection of waders worth checking for species such as Marsh Sandpiper. As you approach the town, after the first roundabout take the next right turn (39.3205N, 3.0006E). This leads to another roundabout where you should turn left and view the saltpans from this road.

4. The Cap de Ses Salines is the most southerly point of mainland Mallorca AND is opposite the islands of Cabrera (page 32) where both Cory's and Balearic Shearwaters breed. Hence this is probably the best place on the mainland to get views of these species. The area around the lighthouse also has potential as a migrant watchpoint, attracting warblers, flycatchers, chats and wheatears to the 'gardens' and a variety of raptors overhead, especially in the autumn; eg Honey Buzzards, Booted Eagles, Marsh Harriers, Black Kites and Hobbies. Just east of Ses Salines village, take the road (39.3385N, 3.0845E) signposted to Cap de Ses Salines and follow it until it ends at the lighthouse after about 9 km. Park and walk to the lighthouse but turn right at the gate (39.2656N, 3.0531E) to follow a path to the shore alongside a wall. Find a space on whichever side of the wall is most sheltered and scan to sea from there. Check the 'gardens' for migrants and maybe walk along the coast in either direction in search of Thekla lark (likely) and Balearic Warbler (difficult). On the way back inland, check the open fields: you should get great views of Stone Curlews and Red-legged Partridges.

5. In my experience, Porto Colom is the easiest place to find Balearic Warbler, even in April when they are quiet (see page 36).

SOUTHERN MALLORCA

N ←

km 0 5

reliable site for Balearic Warbler

Cap Blanc has undisturbed coastal scrub for Balearic Warbler etc

look for Alpine Swifts around San Salvador Monastery

coastal scrub has Balearic Warbler

PORTO COLOM (see page 37)

Petra ↑

FELANITX

SANTANYI

SES SALINES

lighthouse gardens can be good for migrants

④

Cap de Ses Salines possibly best seawatching site on Mallorca

CAMPOS

Salobrar de Campos (see page 35)

②

SA RAPITA

COLONIA DE SAN JORDI (see page 35)

③

To S'Arenal

Cap Blanc lighthouse

①

CALA PI

31

Cabrera

Attraction

A boat trip to Cabrera gives you the best chance of getting close to Balearic and Cory's Shearwaters and gets you to an island which not only has breeding Eleonora's Falcons and a high density of Balearic Warblers, it is also the best place in Mallorca for migrant passerines.

Getting there

There are boats from Portopetro but most visitors arrive from Colonia Sant Jordi. There are two companies but you're more likely to get views of shearwaters by going with Excursions a Cabrera, rather than the speedboat run by Marcabrera. At least in April and May, the crossing can be rough and there are many days on which there is no crossing at all due to the weather. It is therefore important to phone (971 64 90 34) to confirm in advance that the boat is sailing (they usually know the night before). The boat leaves at 10 am but you have to check in at 9.30, so, if you are staying in Port de Pollença, you'll need to set off before 8am.

Notes

1. Visitors to the island have described saling through rafts of Cory's and Balearic Shearwaters sitting on the sea. We had no such luck on 1st May 2012 getting just 4 sightings of Cory's and 1 of Balearic on the crossings there and back. In addition there were plenty of Shags and Yellow-legged Gulls, the occasional Audouin's and a passing Marsh Harrier

2. One of the best spots for Balearic Warbler is just south of the harbour on Cabrera. Walking south from the harbour, you leave the buildings behind and climb up a slight hill. Once over this first rise (39.1501N, 2.9359E) you are in a beautiful area of garrigue habitat with several pairs of Balearic Warbler breeding close to the next 100 metres of track. You are asked not to leave the main track but you really don't need to as the birds can be quite conspicuous, unlike on the rest of Mallorca.

3. The track continues to a beach, behind which is an open grassy area (39.1439N, 2.9373E). This can be simply teeming with migrants - warblers, chats, wheatears, pipits, wagtails, redstarts and flycatchers in far greater numbers than are likely on the mainland. There is every chance of finding a rarer visitor amongst these: Black-eared Wheatear, Collared Flycatcher, Western Olivaceous, Icterine and Melodious Warblers are regularly seen. Subalpine Warblers are relatively easy to find; during April they are mostly of the nominate race but by early May, Moltoni's Subalpine Warbler is more likely.

4. A great place for getting close views of these migrants is at the western corner of the beach where the sea laps over the rocks making shallow pools. Warblers and flycatchers come to bathe there, sometimes joined by other species including, on my visit, Ortolan Bunting.

5. There is a track up the east side of the field which leads to a memorial to French soldiers. En route it passes through excellent habitat where you are likely to find more migrants and Balearic Warbler. Graham Hearl's book suggests that Subalpine Warblers (presumably Moltoni's) breed in this valley but the Spanish ringers we met there said they didn't breed on Cabrera.

6. A Birding Tourist's Guide to Majorca describes some much longer walks you could make on the island but the boat usually leaves at 3 pm so it's more sensible to concentrate on the sites above. Birds such as Peregrine and Eleonora's Falcon may be seen overhead from anywhere, as can passage raptors such as kites, harriers and eagles.

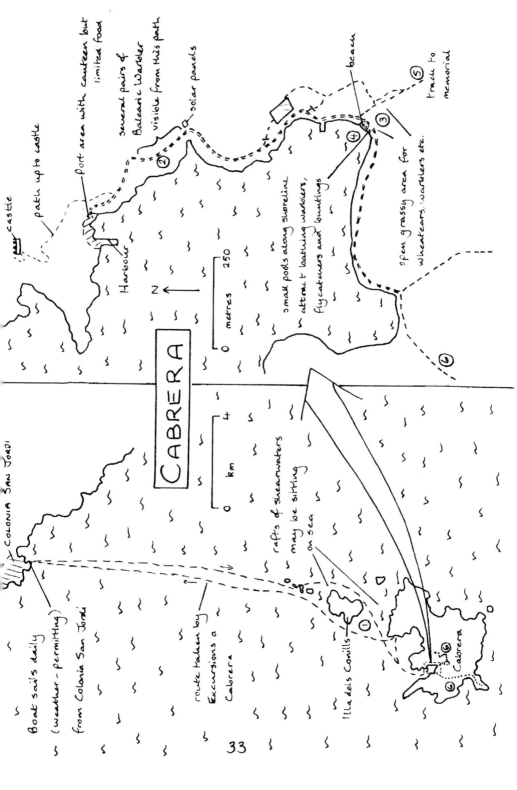

CABRERA

castle

path up to castle

Port area with canteen but limited food

several pairs of Balearic Warbler visible from this path

solar panels

beach

track to memorial

⑤

② ④ ③

Harbour

small pools along shoreline attract bathing warblers, flycatchers and buntings

N

250 metres 0

open grassy area for wheatears, warblers etc.

⑥

COLONIA SAN JORDI

Boat sails daily (weather - permitting) from Colonia San Jordi

km
0

route taken by excursions a Cabrera

rafts of shearwaters may be sitting on sea

Illa dels Conills

①

Calorera

⑥

Salobrar de Campos

Attraction

This site, formerly known as the Salinas de Levante, consists of an extensive area of saltpans with a variety of water levels making this the best site on the island for waders, flamingos and, in winter, cranes. It's great for ducks and herons too and has attracted plenty of Mallorcan rarities.

Getting there

From Felanitx, take the road to Campos then follow signs to Colonia Sant Jordi. At7 km from Campos, when the road reaches the end of a short dual carriageway, the saltpans appear distantly on the right. The best access point is reached by taking the next right (keep straight on when the road bends left at 39.3564N, 3.0164E) to the entrance of the Banys de la Font Santa (a hotel and spa) then following the track to the right towards two palm trees. When you reach a crossroads of tracks (39.3560N, 3.0134E), find somewhere to park then take the left-hand track. This track is known as 'Eddie's Track' after the late Eddie Watkinson who first described its potential for birders. The area can also be viewed from the road to Es Trenc beach.

Notes

1. Eddie's Track takes you between shallow lagoons with varying water levels. You will certainly see lots of Black-winged Stilts, Kentish Plovers and Shelducks which breed abundantly but this is also the best site on the island for Avocet. There can be dozens of waders in these pools such as Ruff, Redshank, Greenshank, Spotted Redshank, Black-tailed Godwit, Little and Temminck's Stints and Curlew Sandpipers. It is particularly good for Marsh Sandpipers: double-figure counts are not unknown.

2. You will notice that there are information boards inside the perimeter of the saltpans. These are part of a 'nature trail' for visitors who pay for a guided walk around the complex. There have been concerns that such walks will increase the disturbance suffered by the birds but, from what I've seen, any birds they put up just settle on a different pool. By joining one of their walks (ask at the salt pan buildings) you would get to see parts of the complex that are otherwise hidden. Access along these paths is prohibited to anyone not on the guided walks.

3. Halfway along Eddie's Track you reach a white building with two windows, a useful landmark. The pools beyond here are usually the best for species such as Greater Flamingo and Spoonbill. At all times you should look for birds flying over, especially terns (marsh terns and Gull-billed), gulls (including, sometimes, Slender-billed, Mediterranean and Little), pratincoles and raptors such as Hobby or Eleonora's Falcon.

4. You can continue as far as a green pumphouse beyond which is an extensive area that sometimes floods and can be good for gulls, terns and pratincoles. This can be one of the best places to look for the Common Cranes which winter on the island; up to 100 have been counted. Also in winter there may be flocks of over 100 Golden Plover.

5. For views of more saltpans, drive back towards Colonia Sant Jordi but turn right on the narrow road (39.3486N, 3.0130E) signposted to Es Trenc. This road passes close to the lagoons; find suitable places to pull in and scan from there. These pools usually have lots of Kentish and other Charadrius Plovers and can have flocks of Calidrid sandpipers such as stints, Dunlin and Curlew Sandpiper. There are usually Short-toed Larks in the fields on the other side of the road.

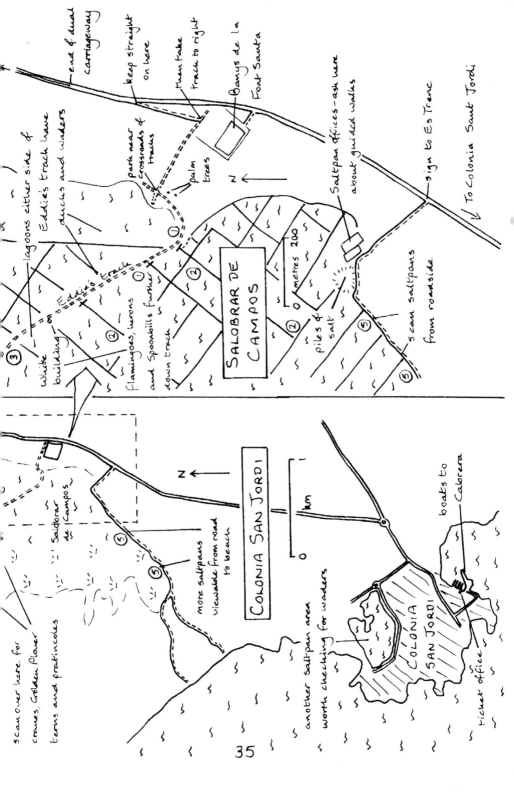

Map 1 — SALOBRAR DE CAMPOS

- end of dual carriageway
- keep straight on here
- Then take track to right
- Banys de la Font Santa
- park near crossroads & tracks
- palm trees
- lagoons either side of Eddie's track have ducks and waders
- Saltpan offices — ask here about guided walks
- sign to Es Trenc
- To Colonia Sant Jordi
- Eddie's track
- Flamingoes, herons and Spoonbills further down track
- White building
- piles of salt
- can saltpans from roadside
- scan saltpans from roadside
- metres 0 — 200
- ① ② ③
- N ←

Map 2 — COLONIA SAN JORDI

- scan over here for cranes, Golden Plover terns and pratincoles
- Salobrar de Campos
- more saltpans viewable from road to beach
- another saltpan area worth checking for waders
- boats to Cabrera
- COLONIA SAN JORDI
- Ticket office
- N ←
- km 0 — 1

35

Porto Colom

Attraction

Best-known as a site where Balearic Warbler is (relatively) easy to find. Other species here include Audouin's Gull, Pallid Swift, Thekla Lark and Stone Curlew.

Getting there

Porto Colom is well-signposted from Felanitx. On reaching Porto Colom, follow signs to the beach ('platja')

Notes

1. At the point where the track to the beach leaves the road (39.4279N, 3.2675E), there is a field on the left which, in the past has been good for larks and migrants such as wheatears and has previously flooded to provide pools for gulls and waders. In 2012 though the grass was rather long and it was much less productive.

2. Park when you get to the rocky bay (s'Algar) and look around for Thekla Larks and Wheatears around the parking area. It may be worth scanning offshore for Cory's and Balearic Shearwaters, especially if there is an onshore wind. Any swifts flying around could be Pallid Swifts and there may be a Shag or two fishing in the bay.

3. About 100 metres south of where the track first meets the shore, there is a little path to the right (from 39.4283N, 3.2722E) towards a copse of pine trees. The area to the right of this path is perhaps the most reliable place in mainland Mallorca for seeing Balearic Warbler. I have made many visits to this site and never failed to find them, in contrast to many other sites I've tried elsewhere. That doesn't mean they are easy, especially in April when they sing very infrequently but with patience you should at least hear one and maybe see a songflight. PLEASE don't use tapes to try to attract these birds; what if everyone else did the same? If it's windy, they won't perch up for long. You'll need to distinguish their songs and calls from Sardinian Warbler and Stonechat which are both numerous.

4. The track continues through the copse of pines to a plateau area where you are likely to find Thekla Lark, Stone Curlew and, possibly, Tawny Pipit.

5. Pallid Swifts breed in the sea cliffs. One place to see them can be reached as follows: follow the road towards the lighthouse ('Far') but turn left where there is a streetlight in a mini roundabout (39.4175N, 3.2719E). Turn left again at the T-junction and follow this road as far as you can to a broad layby (39.4199N, 3.2747E) overlooking the sea. The Pallid Swifts breed in the sea caves, as do Kestrels and, in some years, Peregrines.

6. You're likely to see Audouin's Gull and maybe Shags in the harbour but these are much easier to see at Port de Pollença.

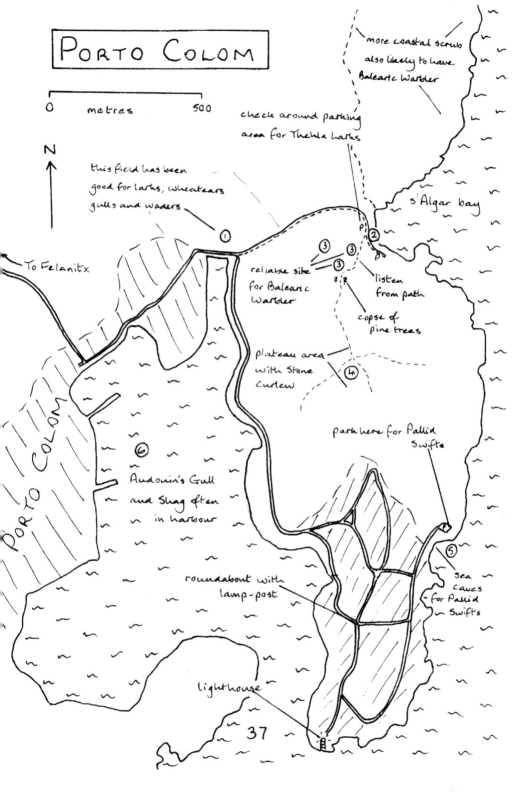

PORTO COLOM

0 metres 500

N

this field has been good for larks, wheatears gulls and waders

①

To Felanitx

more coastal scrub also likely to have Balearic Warbler

check around parking area for Thekla Larks

s'Algar bay

reliable site for Balearic Warbler

③ ③ ③

P ②

listen from path

copse of pine trees

plateau area with Stone Curlew ④

park here for Pallid Swifts

⑥

Audouin's Gull and Shag often in harbour

PORTO COLOM

roundabout with lamp-post

⑤ Sea caves for Pallid Swifts

lighthouse

37